The Piano Works of George Gershwin

Complete Preludes (Ed. Alicia Zizzo)
(Solo Piano)

Alfred's Classic Edition

T0069840

Table of Contents

EXCLUSIVELY DISTRIBUTED BY

HAL•LEONARD®

© 1996 Alfred Music Publishing Co., Inc.
All Rights Reserved.   Printed in USA.
ISBN-10: 0-89724-653-5
ISBN-13: 978-0-89724-653-8

INTRODUCTION TO PERFORMANCE NOTES

In the March 1925 issue of Vanity Fair Magazine, Carl Van Vechten mentions that George Gershwin was working on a collection of twenty four preludes titled "The Melting Pot." Gershwin might very well have been inspired by the twenty four Chopin Preludes which are as diverse from one another as Gershwin's.

The perception of a melting pot as it represented American life in the early part of the twentieth century seems to permeate Gershwin's musical ideas; witness Swanee, Lullaby, Blue Monday, Delicious (the 1931 Screenplay), the Rhapsody in Blue (as the first major American work encompassing cross-cultural musical idioms), An American In Paris, the Preludes (which run the gamut from Klezmar and Jazz to Latin rhythmic motifs), and of course Porgy & Bess.

Although three Preludes were published in 1927, Ira Gershwin confirmed that there were indeed some unpublished pieces intended as Preludes. The mystery of the "lost " Preludes is addressed by Edward Jablonski in his book "Gershwin: A Biography." Mr. Jablonski writes: "The creation or evolution of the collection published as Preludes for piano is shadowy. The pieces Gershwin performed... on December 5, 1926 numbered five." He goes on to confirm that the two "lost" preludes were the Novelette in Fourths and Rubato - to be joined in a later concert by Melody No. 17 (The future Sleepless Night). In my opinion, a resolution to this half-century old puzzle might be found in the fact that in 1925 George Gershwin agreed to allow his friend and colleague Samuel Dushkin to arrange Novelette in Fourths and Rubato as a violin-piano piece which was published as such and titled "Short Story." As for Melody No. 17, Gershwin set this piece aside for later use as a song. In 1946 Kay Swift reworked Sleepless Night, but no lyrics were written for it and it was never published.

There is yet another fragment which bears the name Prelude and is dated January, 1925. It is probably the first prelude Gershwin composed specifically for his collection but was never included in his public performances as it became the opening of the third movement of his forthcoming Concerto in F which premiered in December, 1925.

This edition, the first since 1927, is based upon Gershwin's manuscripts as written in his own hand, with the exception of Sleepless Night in the Kay Swift version, and Preludes Nos. I in B flat and II (Blue Lullaby) for which no manuscripts have been found. The absence of original notation and fully detailed manuscripts presented certain difficulties. For example, we know that Dr. Albert Sirmay, the editor originally assigned to prepare the Preludes for publishing was ill equipped to understand Gershwin's innovative style which removed these pieces so effectively from the 19th century European tradition in which Dr. Sirmay was steeped. As a result, the Preludes were edited with a heavy hand, bringing to them a romanticism out of context with the quickly paced rhythmically steady Gershwin style of the "Roaring Twenties."

In order to facilitate the understanding of this new complete collection of the Preludes, and attempt to remain as authentic as possible given the material at hand, I turned to Leopold Godowsky III for his sage advice as Gershwin family member, gifted composer, and family trustee. At his suggestion, we agreed to create a two-tone edition so that the performer will be able to identify everything originally written in Gershwin's own hand. Much of this material is devoid of pedaling, phrasing, dynamics and the usual attendant interpretive clues, necessitating significant editorial additions. No notes, chords or symbols were altered except in Melody No. 17 which had to be reconstructed from a fragment.

I would like to therefore thank Mr. Godowsky for his wonderful idea to create this two tone score. To Edward Jablonski I owe an unending debt and gratitude, for without his friendship and assistance, this project would not have place." My additional appreciation to Mr. Tony Esposito, editor at Warner Bros. Publications for his unfailing enthusiasm and skilled professionalism in support of my research into this most important aspect of George Gershwin's piano literature, unavailable until now.

One final note on the performance of the Gershwin Preludes: It is crucial to remember that the Preludes are instantly understood by Jazz Performers who often lack the technique to play them, while on the other hand are so often totally misunderstood by classically trained pianists who may have the technique, but apply to them their orientation to the classics. The best approach is to try to identify with the era in which they were written and to maintain a steady pace with few rubatos and special attention to the rhythms - specifically that split-second timing in which what is not played becomes almost more important than what is!

MUSICOLOGICAL HISTORY

As a result of her research, Alicia Zizzo made musicological history with her landmark CD "*Gershwin by Gershwin.*" when she recorded with the Budapest Symphony, the *Concerto in F* in its original form and the *Rhapsody in Blue* in which she performs the 50-plus differences between the manuscript (which is the version that Gershwin himself performed) and the originally published version. That CD also features *Lullaby*, an early Gershwin piece, which she reconstructed from a piano fragment, proving once and for all that it had been originally intended as a piano solo. The recording was produced by Mr. Jablonski.

A second Gershwin CD, featuring Alicia Zizzo's arrangement for piano solo of the *Rhapsody in Blue, Blue Monday, The Six Preludes,* and other never before heard unpublished manuscripts, has also been recorded by her. (Carlton Classics/ Fanfare label, 1996)

Alicia Zizzo has created for publishing, a new edition of a solo-piano suite based upon Gershwin's original sketch of *Blue Monday*, his 1922 opera and first attempt at a major classical composition. Ms. Zizzo has confirmed that *Blue Monday* was indeed Gershwin's seed-cellar for virtually all the classical compositions he subsequently wrote. (The library of Congress recognized this Gershwin piece as one of their more important musicological "finds".) Because Alicia Zizzo has added major new pieces to the Gershwin piano solo catalog, she has significantly expanded his limited classical repertoire.

Warner Bros. and the Gershwin family were so impressed by her research that they decided to make Ms. Zizzo's reconstructions of *Lullaby, Blue Monday, Rhapsody in Blue, The Six Preludes* and other unpublished manuscripts for solo-piano, the first new authentic editions of Gershwin classical material to be published in more than half a century. Until the Gershwin/Zizzo Editions, there were no existing published solo piano scores of any of these pieces. The Gershwin/Zizzo publications are the only editions of this material available worldwide. All this was accomplished with the cooperation of the Gershwin estate and the special blessing of George's sister Frances, and Mr. Tony Esposito at Warner Bros. Publications.

Ms. Zizzo has written about Gershwin's classical repertoire for major publications including *Keyboard Classics, Keyboard Teacher* magazines, *Piano & Keyboard* and others. She is currently writing a book on Gershwin performance techniques. The New York Times, Newsday, The Toronto Star, The Chicago Sun Times and other publications have written articles about Ms. Zizzo's Research.

Significantly, Ms. Zizzo was asked to speak and perform in a documentary entitled *They Changed The World—George Gershwin*, directed by the noted French film maker Alain Resnais, as the American expert on the *Rhapsody in Blue*.

Ms. Zizzo is the first woman to record *Rhapsody in Blue, Lullaby* and the *Concerto in F*. With all this accomplished, Alicia Zizzo is now considered a major new authority on the classical piano music of George Gershwin.

PERFORMANCE NOTES

   A successful interpretation of the Preludes lies in keeping a steady pulse in the bass with few exceptions. Any rubatos or "stolen time" should be worked into this framework. It is also interesting to note Gershwin's use of staccatos under accents and portamentos.

   PRELUDE I (B♭ major): In practicing this prelude, set the metronome at ♪ = 184. This doubled beat helps clarify the famous Gershwin split-second timing in which what is not played is as important as what is played - something easy and familiar to a jazz pianist but often very difficult for the classically trained pianist. The middle eastern "feels" or this Prelude reveals itself in its strong first beat throughout.

   MELODY NO. 17 (A♭): There are two versions contained in this edition. Composed in 1925 as *"Melody No. 17,"* *"Sleepless Night"* was reworked by Kay Swift around 1946 in preparation for a song. Both versions are valid but only the original *Melody No. 17* is in Gershwin's hand and is the one he performed as a Prelude. The melody is found in the eighth notes of the treble clef and is slightly jazzy. The interruption in the middle should be played slightly faster. There is plenty of room for rubatos in this Prelude.

   PRELUDE II (C♯ minor): *Blue Lullaby,* as referred to by Gershwin, has a steady beat throughout and works well when played a little faster than previously thought. Any "stolen time" found in the rubatos should be played more as a "thrust forward" than a ritard (ie: the triplet in the eighth measure can be speeded up slightly with the emphasis on the first note of the triplet, thus allowing for a tiny "breather" without losing the pulse of the piece). The ending of the Prelude becomes clearer if the first note of the third measure before the last (e sharp) is caught by the sostenuto pedal and held to the end, thereby enabling the pianist to control the sustaining pedal as he wishes.

RUBATO (G major): _Rubato_ is "a frank salute to Chopin" according to critic Abbe Niles in his 1926 review of the Preludes. This is true particularly in the middle section which is clearly very romantic. To avoid over-sentimentality, try to play the bass chords without breaking them, (as indicated in the original ms.). The rubatos within this piece should not become extended ritards.

NOVELETTE FOURTHS (E♭): _Novelette in Fourths_ is a Cake Walk; a dance of the 'teens' and twenties in which couples glided along in a stride. Often, there were contests in which the contestants who won received a cake - hence "Cake Walk". This prelude is reminiscent of Debussy's "Golliwog's Cake Walk". It is played rubato and not particularly fast or jazzy as it was composed early, (circa 1919) and not intended as a "rag", although the temptation to play it as one is great.

PRELUDE III (E♭ minor): _Spanish Prelude_, as Gershwin titled it exists in two manuscripts in his hand. This edition is an arrangement containing the first page (the only existing fragment) of an early version which is the one he probably performed and the remainder of a second version which is complete. Even though this Prelude seems to convey several different moods, a strict adherence to the tempo throughout the piece with few, if any, ritards or rubatos (similar to Prelude I) connects them in a scintillating and meaningful way. The different hues of this Prelude can be successfully brought out by emphasizing Gershwin's harmonies in certain places (as indicated) and rhythms in others.

There is yet another fragment which bears the name Prelude and is dated January, 1925. This piece was never performed as a Prelude for it became the opening of the last movement of me Concerto in F, and has been published herein.

The order of the Six Preludes as published here is based upon accounts of his own performances. However, since no real verification exists, the pianist is at liberty to decide individually how to perform them as a group.

* Edward Jablonski; "Gershwin - A Biography" Doubleday Publishing: 1987.

To Bill Daly

Prelude I

(1926)

By GEORGE GERSHWIN
Edited by ALICIA ZIZZO

Allegro ben ritmato e deciso

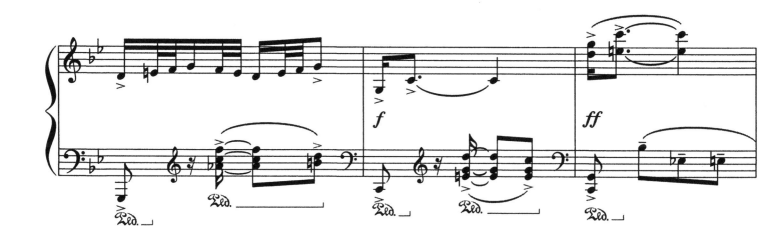

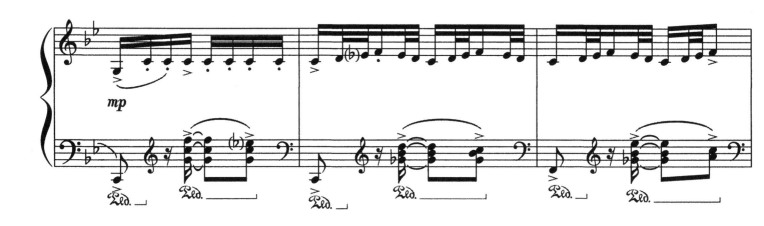

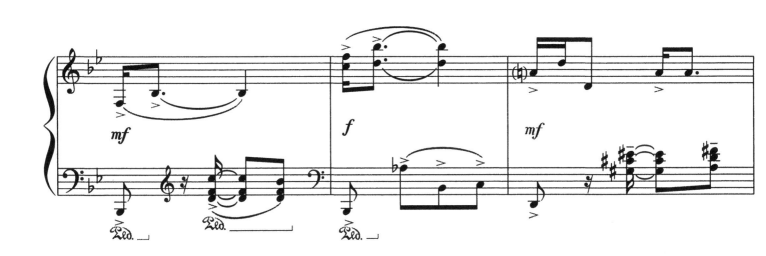

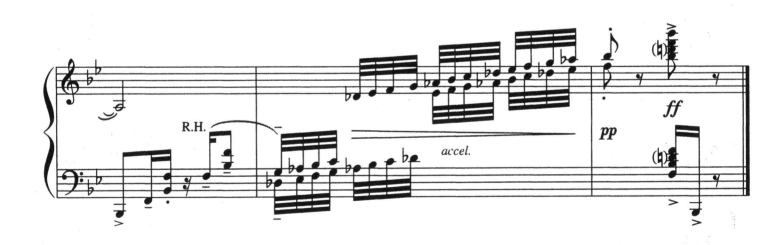

Prelude
(Melody No. 17)
(1925-1926)

By GEORGE GERSHWIN
Edited by ALICIA ZIZZO

PF0895

(A) OSSIA: repeat tied l.h. notes

Prelude
(Rubato)
(1923)

By GEORGE GERSHWIN
Edited by ALICIA ZIZZO

* Although I is indicated in the original manuscript, breaking or "rolling" the bass is easier to play and may be the way George Gershwin actually played Rubato.

Prelude II
(Blue Lullaby)
(1926)

By GEORGE GERSHWIN
Edited by ALICIA ZIZZO

*OSSIA: Do not break chords. On third beat, play B♯ with R.H.

Largamente con moto
Optional: REVERSE HANDS
slightly jazzy

*OSSIA: Slightly accelerate ending

Prelude
(Novelette in Fourths)
(ca. 1919)

By GEORGE GERSHWIN
Edited by ALICIA ZIZZO

*Tempo rubato

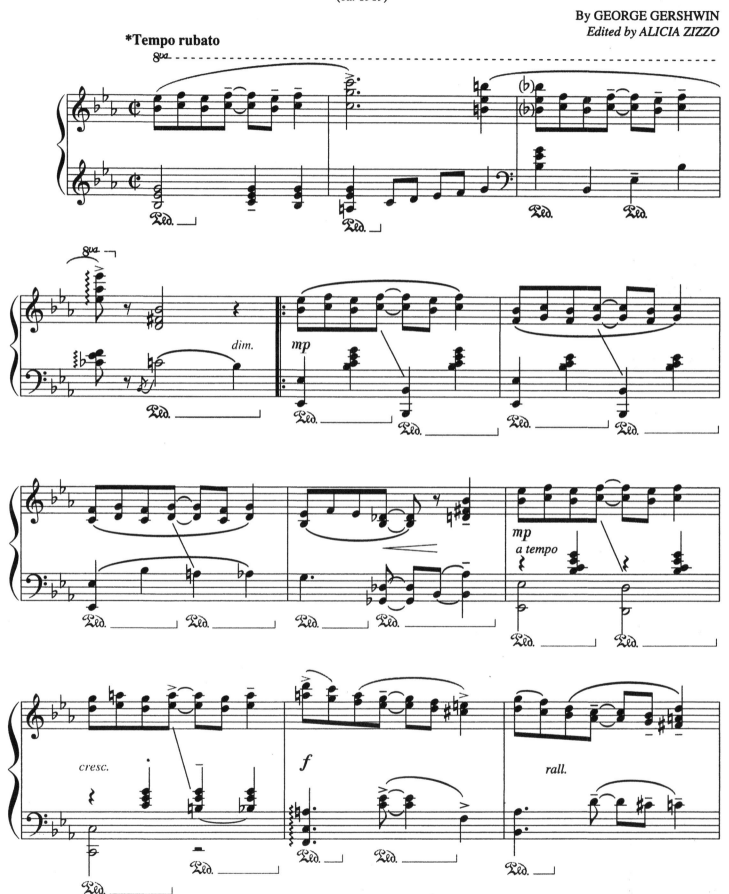

* As indicated in original MS.

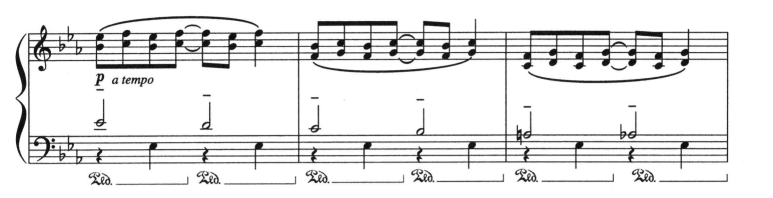

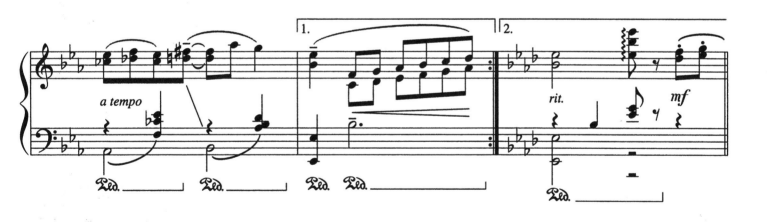

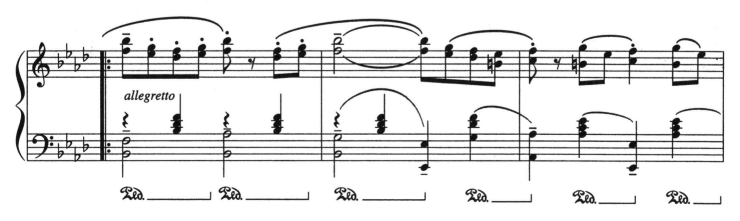

Prelude III
(Spanish Prelude)

By GEORGE GERSHWIN
Edited by ALICIA ZIZZO

* "Agitato" is the only tempo indication given in original ms.
Bars 5-20 are edited according to the first of 2 original manuscripts (only a one page fragment exists of the first original).
The second original was the one submitted for publishing and is used for the remainder of this prelude.

** Cb appears as a sixteenth note in first ms. and as an eighth note in second, therefore: optional.

*** In second original MS., the half note Eb is written as a sixteenth and is repeated in second beat.

Ⓐ As in first original manuscript

OSSIA: (As in first published edition and second MS.)

Ⓐ a C♮ indicated in the original - However, George Gershwin plays C♭ in his recordings. The pianist therefore has 2 options here. If possible, this and following L.H. chords should not be broken.

Ⓐ OSSIA: Play sixteenth as in beginning

Prelude (Fragment)
(Used as 3rd movement of Concerto in F)
(January 1925)

By GEORGE GERSHWIN
Edited by ALICIA ZIZZO

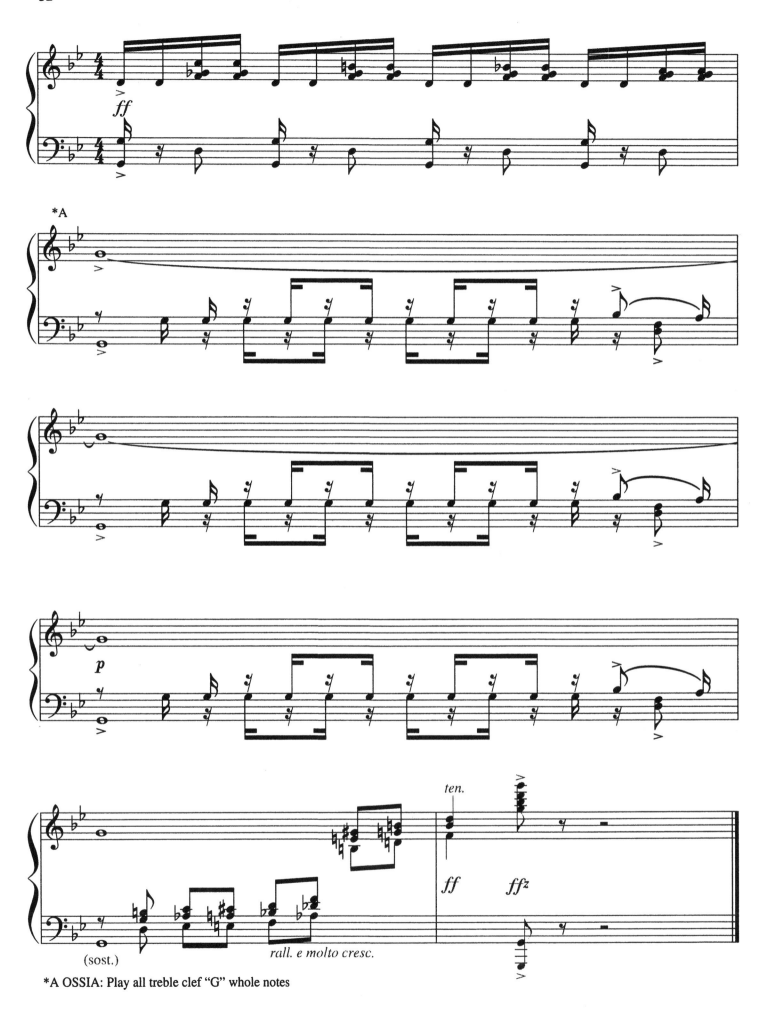

*A OSSIA: Play all treble clef "G" whole notes

Prelude
(Sleepless Night*)
(1946)
(Kay Swift Version)

By GEORGE GERSHWIN
Edited by ALICIA ZIZZO

* This 1946 version of SLEEPLESS NIGHT was written in Kay Swift's hand, as she prepared it to become a song. The earlier, 1925 Melody No. 17, was the piece Gershwin wrote and performed as a prelude in 1926.

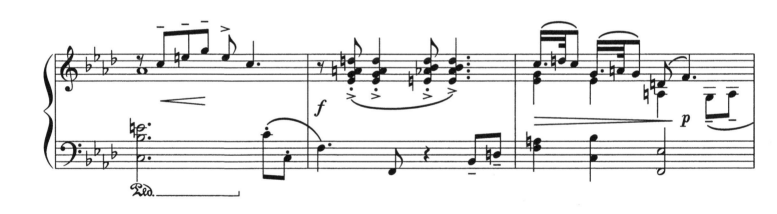

BIOGRAPHY

Alicia Zizzo's musical artistry has taken her to stages in London (The Barbican Center), Amsterdam (The Concerto), Vienna (The Musikverein), Budapest (The Vigado, with the Budapest Symphony), Warsaw (The Ostrovsky Palace for the Chopin Society), New York (Avery Fisher and Carnegie Hall), as well as to Edinburgh, Glasgow, Chicago (with the Chicago Sinfonietta), Germany (the Jaguar in Concert series), and other major venues.

Alicia Zizzo's gifts were recognized early by the legendary Dimitri Mitropolus who referred to her as "An extraordinary talent ... with a musical perception which is not often heard." This accolade came after her Carnegie Hall recital debut at age 11. As a prodigy, she was a pupil of Dr. Carlos Buhler. Following in the tradition of his own great teachers, Alfred Corot and Ferruccio Busoni, Dr. Buhler trained Alicia to play in the grand Virtuoso style of these venerable masters.

Alicia Zizzo's scholarly commitment has been particularly in the research and restoration of the classical piano literature of George Gershwin. Specifically, Alicia Zizzo's goal has been to enhance his remarkably small classical piano solo repertoire. Working with the Library of Congress and leading Gershwin scholar Edward Jablonski, she has spent the last several years investigating the composer's original classical piano manuscripts. Her research into the *Rhapsody in Blue* alone found more than 30 differences between his manuscripts and their published edition.

What has distinguished Ms. Zizzo's work is that she approaches Gershwin's manuscripts not with the objective of making another arrangement of his melodies as so many musicians have already done, but rather to literally reconstruct from fragments, sketches and partially completed scores, Gershwin's own material, thus creating brand new Gershwin compositions while at the same time never losing sight of his purity and intent.

As a result of her research, Alicia Zizzo made musicological history with her landmark CD *"Gershwin by Gershwin"*, when she recorded with the Budapest Symphony, the *Concerto in F* in its original form and the *Rhapsody in Blue* in which she performs the 60-plus differences between the manuscript (which is the version that Gershwin himself performed) and the originally published version. That CD also features *Lullaby*, an early Gershwin piece, which she reconstructed from a piano fragment.

A second Gerswin CD, *"Rediscovered Gershwin"* featuring Alicia Zizzo's arrangement for piano solo of the *Rhapsody in Blue, Blue Monday, The Six Preludes,* and other never before heard unpublished manuscripts, has also been recorded by her, for Carlton Classics (Pickwick)/Fanfare Records (1996).

Alicia Zizzo created a new edition of a solo-piano suite based upon Gershwin's original sketch of *Blue Monday*, his 1922 opera and first attempt at a major classical composition. Ms. Zizzo has confirmed that *Blue Monday* was indeed Gershwin's seed-cellar for the *Rhapsody in Blue*, and virtually all the classical compositions he subsequently wrote. (The library of Congress recognized this Gershwin piece as one of their more important musicological "finds".) Because Alicia Zizzo has added major new pieces to the Gershwin piano solo catalog, she has significantly expanded his limited classical repertoire.

Warner Bros. and the Gershwin family decided to make Ms. Zizzo's reconstructions of *Lullaby, Blue Monday, Rhapsody in Blue, The Six Preludes* and other unpublished manuscripts for solo-piano, the first new authentic editions of Gershwin classical material to be published in more than half a century. Until the Gershwin/Zizzo Editions, there were no existing published solo piano scores of any of these pieces. The Gershwin/Zizzo publications are the only editions of this material available worldwide. All this was accomplished with the cooperation of the Gershwin estate and the special blessing of George's sister Frances.

Ms. Zizzo has written about Gershwin's classical repertoire for major publications.